a poor future

Peter Townsend is Emeritus Professor of Social Policy at the University of Bristol. In a series of research papers and international seminars he contributed to the preparation of the 1995 World Summit for Social Development and was attached to the UN co-ordinating committee during the Summit. In the 1990s he has also worked for the European Union, the International Labour Office and the US Government on issues concerned with poverty, deprivation and health.

Professor Townsend is perhaps best known for his book *Poverty in the United Kingdom* (1979) and his co-authorship of the Black Report, *Inequalities in Health* (1980). In the 1990s he has been writing and teaching on questions of international poverty and health. His most recent book is *The International Analysis of Poverty* (1993).

In 1994–95 he has also worked with Oxfam, One World Action, War on Want and Save the Children. He is Chairman of the Disability Alliance (1974–96). He is also President of the Child Poverty Action Group in the UK (formerly its Chairman 1968–89). After being elected for 31 years successively to the Executive Committee of the Fabian Society (and its Chairman 1965–66) he is now vice-President.

a poor future

can we counter growing poverty in Britain and across the world?

Peter Townsend

in association with
The Friendship Group

Published in Great Britain 1996 by Lemos & Crane
20 Pond Square
Highgate
London N6 6BA
Telephone 0181 348 8263

in association with

The Friendship Group
17–19 Braithwaite Road
Birmingham B11 1LB

ISBN 1-898001-29-4

A CIP catalogue record for this book is available from
the British Library.

Cover design by Richard Newport
Text design and formatting by The Design Works, Reading
Printed by Biddles, Guildford

for Ben

contents

tables

foreword

by John Crawley

Chief Executive of The Friendship Group, Birmingham

A Poor Future is an extended and annotated version of the lecture delivered by Professor Peter Townsend which was jointly sponsored by Friendship and our associated charity, Friendship Community Trust, in memory of Sarah Gibbs.

Professor Townsend starts from the international context for poverty. He reminds us that we can neither understand many of the structural forces underlying poverty here in Britain, nor in an era of global markets hope to combat them, without starting from this perspective. He supports the UN's call for 'national poverty eradication plans to address the structural causes of poverty, encompassing action on the local, national, subregional and international levels'. The statistics on the trend of poverty in the 1980s and 1990s he cites are shocking enough but he also reminds us that poverty depends not only on income but also access to services.

Whilst Peter Townsend bases his case on hard facts and analysis, he also articulates the moral imperative for practical and co-ordinated action at all levels, international, national and local. At the local level, this imperative must inspire voluntary and charitable organisations like Friendship and the individuals who drive them. Friendship, as our name suggests, is committed to such practical support to individuals and their communities. As a social business, we now aim to set our core services (housing and community care) within a broader strategic framework of support for local communities, assisting in their regeneration. This may call for new services critical to alleviating poverty, such as child care, training and employment opportunities. But of equal importance is the need for all businesses, social and commercial, which recognise their wider social responsibilities, to assess the broader effectiveness and impact on poverty and inequality of their core activities. This process of evaluation, sometimes termed social audit, starts from questions such as: how far are local communities in need benefiting from our activities, our investment and our presence as a local employer and purchaser of goods and services? The impact of such social audits, if applied on a widespread and consistent basis by all organisations, could be significant in tackling and reversing some of the problems and trends which entrench poverty and disadvantage in our social system.

We like to describe ourselves as an open and learning organisation; that means listening to other people as we develop our own ideas for combating poverty and disadvantage. Peter Townsend has inspired us to redouble our efforts; I hope this book plants the seed of change elsewhere as well.

introduction

Recent debates about poverty in the United Kingdom have become thoroughly confused. On the one hand the Government has signed a United Nations declaration and programme for action on social development which confirms the existence of absolute poverty in 'all countries'[1] and which, irrespective of measures to specify and remove it, is part of an even more widely shared problem of 'overall' poverty.

On the other hand, the Government refuses to accept that 'poverty' in Britain has any real meaning and, if it has, that much of it is temporary or inconsequential for those concerned.

This is a paradox which demands to be investigated and explained. I shall try to explain it as a necessary basis for a call for more scientific, educational and political action to grapple with

---

[1] UN, 1995, p. 57

what might properly be regarded as the greatest structural problem of our time.

I will now introduce the key statements which I am hoping to put together. Financial hardship in the UK population is more severe than generally supposed. Poverty, in different meanings, has been getting more extensive at the same time as the prosperity of the rich has substantially grown. The social consequences for everyone and not just poor people themselves are coming more widely to public notice. Those consequences will lead to levels of social instability which will be difficult for all but the most ruthless and authoritarian of governments to control. An alternative and more optimistic conclusion is hard to justify: there are few signs that the structural trend is likely to be halted, still less reversed. These statements apply around the world, though they apply in lesser or greater degree.

They apply most strongly to Eastern Europe and the republics of the former Soviet Union. They apply just as strongly to many Third World countries, and to some rich countries, especially the United States, but less strongly to such acknowledged 'welfare state' countries as Germany, the Netherlands and Sweden. If the trend is international then the causes of that trend are international as well as also national, regional and local. Consequently there have to be well-laid international as well as national, regional and local plans to deal with the problem and mitigate the disastrous prospects.

a national paradox

Let me first explain the national paradox. Too little attention has been given in 1995 and 1996 to the agreement reached at the Copen- ✗ hagen Summit on Social Development in March 1995.[2] The summit was called because many governments were becoming restive with the lack of progress in reducing the gap in living standards between rich and poor countries and, despite the blandishments of the international financial agencies, the growth of rock-bottom forms of poverty. At the same time, there were other, associated, problems of unemployment and social disintegration which were clamouring for equally urgent attention by governments.

Globalisation had been driven in part by high hopes of shared greater prosperity but the rapid processes of change and adjustment had

---

[2] UN, 1995 and 1996

been accompanied by more poverty, unemployment and social disintegration, too
often resulting in 'isolation, marginalisation
and violence. The insecurity that many people,
especially vulnerable people, face about the
future – their own and their children's – is
intensifying'.[3]

The report repeatedly emphasised that the gap
between rich and poor within both developed
and developing societies was widening, just as
the gap between developed and developing
societies was also widening. Calling world
attention to this dual structural phenomenon
is perhaps the most notable achievement of the
summit – whatever might be said in criticism
of the attempts in the text to please different
governments and satisfy their conflicting
objectives.

What does the agreed report convey? More
than one billion people in the world live in
abject poverty, many going hungry every day.

---

[3] UN, 1995, pp. 5–6

Among them there are disproportionately more women, blacks, children, single parents, unemployed, disabled and elderly. Old diseases are getting re-established and new ones provoking alarm. In large tracts of the world environmental problems are beyond control. Civil war and betrayal of human rights now apply to an increased number of countries. Measured unemployment is more extensive than it was. The interrelated character of the problem draws repeated references.

Thus: 'The major cause of the continued deterioration of the global environment is the unsustainable pattern of consumption and production, particularly in industrialised countries, which is a matter of grave concern, aggravating poverty and imbalances'. [4]

What did the UN say about poverty? As many as 117 governments signed the declaration and programme of action. Governments should

---

[4] UN, 1995, p. 6

make greater 'public efforts to eradicate absolute poverty and reduce overall poverty substantially' by promoting sustained economic growth within the context of sustainable development and by 'formulating or strengthening, preferably by 1996, and implementing national poverty eradication plans to address the structural causes of poverty, encompassing action on the local, national, sub-regional, and international levels. These plans should establish, within each national context, strategies and affordable time-bound goals and targets for the substantial reduction of overall poverty and the eradication of absolute poverty... Each country should develop a precise definition and assessment of absolute poverty.' [5]

The UN text makes extensive reference to employment and social integration policies. Indeed, the conquest of poverty, the goal of full

---

[5] UN, 1995, pp. 60–61

employment, and the fostering of stable, safe and just societies were the three themes at the summit and became the three pledges endorsed by all countries.

'absolute' and 'overall' poverty

The UN approach allows us to sharpen what might be done in the UK. Absolute poverty is defined as 'a condition characterised by severe deprivation of basic human needs, including food, safe drinking water, sanitation facilities, health, shelter, education and information. It depends not only on income but also on access to services'. [6]

Overall poverty takes various forms including, 'Lack of income and productive resources to ensure sustainable livelihoods; hunger and malnutrition; ill health; limited or lack of access to education and other basic services; increased morbidity and mortality from illness; homelessness and inadequate housing; unsafe environments and social discrimination and exclusion. It is also characterised by lack of participation in decision-making and in civil,

---

[6] UN, 1995, p. 57

social and cultural life. It occurs in all countries: as mass poverty in many developing countries, pockets of poverty amid wealth in developed countries, loss of livelihoods as a result of economic recession, sudden poverty as a result of disaster or conflict, the poverty of low-wage workers, and the utter destitution of people who fall outside family support systems, social institutions and safety nets. [7]

The British Government is therefore expected to prepare a national poverty eradication plan, Х and has apparently agreed to do so. Yet it seems to be dodging the implications and in more than a year has taken little, if any, action to fulfil the agreement. I have quoted some of the detailed terms of the agreement, and to show that they are not just stray afterthoughts or marginal to the proposed strategy it is necessary to quote the two most relevant commitments expressed at the start of the international agreement.

---

[7] UN, 1995, p. 57

'**Commitment 2:** We commit ourselves to the goal of eradicating poverty in the world, through decisive national actions and international cooperation, as an ethical, social, political and economic imperative of humankind.' [8]

'**Commitment 4:** We commit ourselves to promoting social integration by fostering societies that are stable, safe and just and that are based on the promotion and protection of all human rights, as well as on non-discrimi-

espect for diversity, equality

idarity, security, and partic-

le, including disadvantaged

oups and persons.' [9]

ng action taken by different

gencies in the wake of the

mit. It has begun publishing

[9] UN, 1995, p. 18

a new review entitled *Social Policy and Social Progress* [10], and a number of governments, including the Netherlands and Norway [11], have embarked on substantial programmes of action.

---

[10] See, for example, Meereboer, 1994

[11] UN, 1996

British obduracy

But how will the British Government square the circle? Given its acceptance of the agreement, and despite its refusal to take poverty in the UK seriously, what will it do?

The problem goes back to the debate in the 1970s and 1980s. Britain published a series of statistics on low income, showing how many in the population, irrespective of earnings and benefits, had incomes below the going rates of Supplementary Benefit or what became 'Income Support' at the end of the 1980s. This series was abandoned in favour of a new series about the incomes of households below average income. [12]

---

[12] DHSS, 1988; DSS, 1990–1995; Townsend, 1993a; Johnson and Webb, 1990a and 1990b

This change was widely opposed, and the relevant all-Party House of Commons Select Committee was a prominent opponent.[13] The value of the earlier series was that even if it was not based on operational criteria of 'poverty' at least it showed how many people, and what kind of people, did not have sufficient incomes to match what government paid out as minimum benefits.

What is remarkable is that then and now the Government ignored international practice. The World Bank takes the concept seriously – even if it refuses to adopt scientific criteria and thereby concede the need for a higher poverty line than the 'dollar a day' standard, or two dollars a day in Latin America, which they arbitrarily and irrationally use. [14] The European Union has continued to produce research and official statistics describing the pheno-

---

[13] See, for example, Social Services Committee, 1988 and 1989; and Social Security Committee, 1991

[14] World Bank, 1990 and 1993; Townsend, 1994

menon [15], even if it has resorted to unsatis-
factory indicators like half average household
income[16] or, in the case of Eurostat, half
average expenditure, for reasons of practical
convenience [17].

And the United States has a long history of
measured assessments of trends in poverty.[18]
The US National Academy of Science sponsored a major review of the measurement of
poverty, resulting in a 500 page publication in
1995. [19]

Successive British Prime Ministers and
Secretaries of State for Social Security in the

---

[15] Commission of the European Communities, 1991;
Robbins, 1994; Smeeding, O'Higgins, Rainwater and
Atkinson, 1989

[16] Illustrated in elaborate secondary analyses like that of
Smeeding, O'Higgins and Rainwater, 1989

[17] Eurostat, 1990 and 1994

[18] See, for example, US Department of Commerce, 1992;
Committee on Ways and Means, 1994

[19] Citro and Michael, 1995

post-war years have obstinately resisted international conventions as well as scientific work. One of the most revealing examples is provided by John Moore, Secretary of State for Social Security in 1989.[20] He accepted that poverty had existed in the nineteenth century but denied that it existed in the latter part of the twentieth century. Relative definitions were in his opinion 'bizarre.' The numbers said to be in poverty were arbitrary or exaggerated. They represented 'an attempt to discredit our real economic achievement in protecting and improving the living standards of our people ... Their purpose in calling poverty what is in reality simply inequality is so that they can call western material capitalism a failure'.[21] Whatever the arguments about others' definitions and measures he, and subsequent Secretaries of State, refused to put forward definitions or standards for the UK.

---

[20] Moore, 1989

[21] Moore, 1989, pp. 12–14

There were also open disagreements with fellow Cabinet Ministers. Thus, Ian Gilmour has given in an autobiography a graphic and sensitive account of the growth of poverty in the 1980s.[22] The paradox has been made more absurd in recent pronouncements from Peter Lilley.[23] It is a shabby and disreputable episode in the history of British statistics as well as government. It deserves to be resolved quickly. Britain must align its research and statistical reports with the best scientific international practice.[24] The distinction drawn by the UN in the Copenhagen agreement between 'absolute' and 'overall' poverty offers the chance of making a fresh approach.

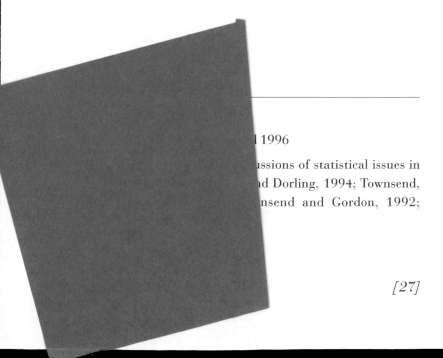

1 1996

ıssions of statistical issues in
ıd Dorling, 1994; Townsend,
ınsend and Gordon, 1992;

the severity of poverty

The Government's unwillingness to treat the
X concept of poverty seriously and to seek to give
operational definitions has affected the entire
production of information about hardship and
low income, both by government and indepen-
dently. It has even led to the pulling of punches
by independent organisations and campaigning bodies. A number of them hesitate to
call sharp attention to expert scientific evidence
of deteriorating social conditions, and
adequately represent public and professional
opposition and indeed abhorrence of those
conditions, for fear of being accused of taking
up 'politically' motivated positions unacc-
eptable, for example, to the Charity
Commissioners, and to a variety of quangos
appointed by the Government.

The Government has encouraged us to become
mealy-mouthed about the enlargement of
poverty and has undermined confidence in
those who are professionally concerned to chart
the effects and discover solutions. There is good

science and bad science but science there has to be in defining, measuring, explaining and disposing of the phenomenon of poverty.

Is there evidence that the problem is worse than it was nearly two decades ago? A start can be made with information released by the Government, but to which no attention has been drawn. Table 1 provides an illustration. The Government has produced statistics on two rock-bottom measures of low income. [25] One of these measures is half the median (i.e. the middle) ranked income of the poorest tenth of the population in 1979. The other measure is half the average household income in that year.

Because there has been continued economic growth in the 17 years since 1979, almost the entire national population might have been expected to have easily surmounted these two historical baselines (when measured at 1995 prices). I know of no comparable period of the twentieth century when the purchasing power

---

[25] See, for example, DSS, 1995a, Appendix 11

Table 1 Children and adults in households below 1979 fixed income thresholds (after housing costs)

Children		
1979 standard	*1979*	*1992–93*
Below 1979 poorest decile median	860,000	1,180,000
Below 50% of 1979 average income	1,430,000	1,940,000

Adults		
1979 standard	*1979*	*1992–93*
Below 1979 poorest decile median	2,000,000	2,970,000
Below 50% of 1979 average income	3,850,000	4,100,000

Note: The increase in children below 1979 low-income standards is not due to an increase in the child population. The size of that population has in fact fallen and official statistics show that if the populations were standardised the *proportionate* increase in children in households with incomes below 1979 levels would be larger than shown in the table. *Source:* DSS, *Households Below Average Income*, London, HMSO, Tables 11–2 and 11–5. Written answer to Jean Corston, MP, *Hansard*, 18 July 1995, cols 1089–1090

of the poorest sections of the population not
only failed to grow, but slipped back. In fact,
as the table shows, there were more children
below the 1979 standards of low income in the
early 1990s than there were in 1979. The same
is true of adults.

Why is the change so dramatic? Illustrations
can be given for different poor families. Among
the poorest tenth of households in 1979 a
married couple with two children aged three
and eight had a disposable income after
housing costs, at April 1995 prices, of £106 per
week. Had such a family enjoyed the national
average percentage improvement in income in
the years to 1992–93 then they would have had
an income, also at April 1995 prices, in that
recent year of £144 per week – representing an
increase of £38 per week or £1,976 a year.

In fact such a family experienced a fall in
income of £18 per week or £936 a year. Larger
families have been even worse affected. Thus, a
couple with three children aged eleven, sixteen
and seventeen in that poorest tenth might have
expected to increase their income of £106 per

week by £55 or £2,860 a year. In fact they had to stomach a fall of £26 a week or £1,352 a year.

The growth in the numbers of unemployed and elderly outside the workforce does not explain the increase in the number of people having less than 1979 standards of low income, shown in Table 1. This increase includes people in work, especially the self-employed, but also part-time and full-time employees.

the growth of poverty

One reason for the increase in poverty is therefore the fall in low earnings as well as the persistence of large-scale unemployment. Second, for major sections of the population Income Support is of less value than it used to be. The numbers in the population with incomes below the 1979 equivalent of Income Support, or directly dependent on successor schemes of Income Support, have grown substantially. Table 2, on page 34, gives a single (official) account of that growth.

A number of measures were introduced to lower the real value of Income Support. After the introduction of the new scheme in 1988 a couple with two children under the age of eleven were found to have lost £3.60 per week, and a lone person with one child under eleven 95 pence, whereas a single person with disabilities lost £8.75.[26]

---

[26] Oppenheim, 1990a

*Table 2 **Increase in numbers of children
dependent on Supplementary Benefit and
Income Support 1979–1994***

Numbers of children dependent on Income Support			
Year	*Under 10 yrs*	*10–13*	*14–16*
1979	574,000	236,000	135,000
1989	1,463,000	384,000	250,000
1994	2,080,000	629,000	369,000

Numbers of children dependent on Housing Benefit without Income Support			
Year	*Under 10 yrs*	*10–13*	*14–16*
1989	187,000	69,000	51,000
1994	284,000	104,000	61,000

Source: Written answer to Jean Corston, MP, *Hansard*, 19 July 1995, cols 1477–1480

Income Support for 16 and 17-year-olds was withdrawn, and payments for young unemployed people under 25 greatly reduced. Pensioners and disabled people found that additional weekly allowances and single grants were drastically cut. The introduction of the Social Fund has also reduced the real value of Income Support to hundreds of thousands of people. Exceptional needs grants were largely replaced by loans, and this has meant that instead of being able to top-up Income Support for exceptional problems, at the discretion of the administering authority, families lose part of their miserly weekly Income Support to re-pay a loan. Beveridge's meagre subsistence has been replaced by Scrooge.

There have been dozens of small changes in the social security system to reduce entitlement to income. Clearly we need a more highly developed sense of strategic priorities and a more coherent method of tracking proportionate effects. For example, there has been a particularly detrimental fall in the living standards of many women and children. The factors include the abolition of the universal maternity grant; childcare costs cannot be offset against earnings for Income Support claimants, as they could under supplementary benefit; child benefit was frozen in value during certain years and is of lower value than in 1979; entitlement to free school meals was absorbed into Family Credit payments with smaller real value; the restructuring of the State Earnings-Related Pension Scheme has greatly weakened entitlements for women; and the 1995 Budget included the freezing of the lone-parent premium and one-parent benefit.[27]

Third, the sharp increase in the severity of poverty is illustrated by the homeless. These are people who cannot afford rents for housing or hostels. In 1979 55,530 households fell within the official measure of the homeless. In 1994 it was 122,660. The official measure excludes both those who are deemed 'intentionally homeless' and those defined as having

---

[27] See Oppenheim and Harker, 1996, pp. 109–110

no 'priority need'. As most adults without children are not in 'priority need', the unofficial homeless are hard to estimate, and no serious efforts have been made by Government to clarify the size and seriousness of the problem.

Worse, the 1995 White Paper 'Our Future Homes' proposed to set housing benefit below market rents, further restrict exceptional hardship payments, limit housing benefit for people under 25 to the cost of a bedsitting room – to apply from October 1996 – and to change the local authority responsibility for housing the priority homeless to cover temporary accommodation for only twelve months.

As one Salvation Army report explains, 'London has a shanty town as large as might be expected in a Latin American city, but it is hidden. People live illegally in squats or in cramped, badly equipped hotels and crowded hostels. If they do not fall into a group that the government recognises as having a special need, or they cannot locate one of the very few spare spaces indoors, they find they have no choice but to survive on the streets'. [28]

The poverty affecting many homeless people in Britain is properly of a kind which can be described as 'absolute' poverty in the sense ⚔ advocated by the United Nations. Their numbers must surely be complemented by many thousands in poor rented conditions, especially the most run-down housing estates, and scratching a living to pay off severe debt, or earn eligibility to some income. Independent research reminds us of the poverty of prisoners' families; young people between 16 and 18 who are living alone and trying to fend for themselves [29]; and the failure of many families, particularly mothers and children to secure a diet sufficient to cover the Department of Health's Dietary Recommended Values. One research team from the John Moores' University of Liverpool, for example, found

---

[28] Canter et al, 1995

[29] Sparks, 1995, pp. 52–53

that as many as 30 per cent were failing to spend enough to cover average necessary nutrients.[30]

The connections between poor health and poverty are strongly established[31], and case studies of problems of meeting even the basic needs of disabled children and disabled elderly are now voluminous. This material should be brought together responsibly by government to find what is going wrong[32]; but also how national strategies of social development might be improved.

The churches have of course been playing a more and more prominent role in calling attention to increasing impoverishment. The National Poverty Hearing in March 1996 at Church House Westminster showed what an

---

[30] Sparks, 1995, p. 57

[31] Benzeval et al., 1992 and 1995; Wilkinson, 1994 and 1996; Holtermann, 1995; Grayson et al., 1992; and Kumar 1993

[32] Models of such good editorial work will be found, for example, in Kempson, 1996

influential role they can play. The churches have been derided as politically motivated 'whistle-blowers' when they are trying to warn of an increasingly serious social evil.

official and independent evidence

I have tried to point out that there is official evidence of the growth in severity of poverty – as can be shown from statistics on unemployment, earnings, Income Support, and homelessness. This evidence is often watered down, tucked away in obscure corners or juxtaposed with evidence which seems to contradict it. A glass three-quarters full which becomes half full can be described as half full and half empty.

This helps to explain how important are complementary independent studies. These are usually produced by charities, churches, research institutes and campaigning groups. [33]

---

[33] See, for example, Benzeval, Judge and Solomon, 1992; Berthoud and Kempson, 1992; Bradshaw, 1990; Bradshaw and Holmes, 1989; Cohen, Coxhall, Craig and Sadiq-Sangster, 1992; Craig and Glendinning, 1990; Gordon and Pantazis, 1995; Kempson, 1996; Kempson, Bryson and Rowlandson, 1994; Kumar, 1993; Lee and Townsend, 1994; Marsh and Mckay, 1993; Oppenheim and Harker, 1996; Sinfield, 1993; Wilkinson, 1995

There are a large number of local authority studies of poverty as well which can be added to the list. [34]

Many such reports are case-studies of minorities or local communities. Usually they are smaller in scale than the national data produced from government administrative statistics and random sample surveys. Usually they cost a lot less than national investigations and although they are frequently dismissed by Government ministers because they apply to small numbers they can be more reliable because they are much more rounded and less superficial than many government reports – in the sense that social indicators drawn from the Census or from expenditure and income surveys can be very limited in what they portray about deprivation, for instance.

A study sponsored by Barnado's, for example, called attention to growing child poverty and

---

[34] See, for example, the report on the city of Birmingham: Baker, 1989; and the bibliography of local studies of poverty in Grayson, Hobson and Smith, 1992

concluded, 'Financial hardship increases the risks of family conflict and also of emotional disturbance and delinquency in children... Greater material insecurity, a sense of injustice and a growth of anti-social tendencies take their toll throughout society'.[35] A major report from the National Children's Bureau declared, 'Our review of evidence... indicates the continuation of an unmistakeable trend towards sharply rising child poverty since 1979'.[36] The report went on to list worsening factors and pointed out that at the World Summit on Children in November 1989 Margaret Thatcher committed the UK to the UN Convention on the Rights of the Child, adding, 'The well-being of children requires political action at the highest level. We make a solemn commitment to give priority to the rights of children'.[37] And a review of 31 studies by the Joseph Rowntree Foundation showed how

---

[35] Wilkinson, 1994, p. 64

[36] Kumar, 1993, p. 187

[37] Kumar, 1993, p. 197; and also see Van Bueren, 1994

families improvise when they hit financial crisis, adults – especially women – who sometimes either go without food to support children or turn off the heating in winter to avoid getting into debt.[38]

A 1993 report by UNICEF entitled *Child Neglect in Rich Nations* explained why some of the richest nations on earth 'have short-changed children'. The agency had spotlighted the particularly high proportion of children in the United States and the United Kingdom who experienced poverty. There were such wide differences between the UK or the US and most European countries that a European model of child welfare was contrasted with a 'neglect-filled' Anglo-American model. The 'swelling tide of child neglect has potentially disastrous consequences... Unless countries like the US and the UK invest in their children on a new

---

[38] Kempson, 1996, pp. 23–35; for a vivid review of other evidence see Cohen, Coxall, Craig and Sadiq-Sangster, 1994; and Bradshaw and Holmes, 1989

and massive scale, a burgeoning human capital deficit will trigger an economic tailspin' .[39]

The national reports from non-government sources document the living standards and experiences of scores, hundreds or thousands of people in different areas of the country. Although they can be said to supplement our knowledge of poverty in many different ways their importance is best conveyed by a compensating 'depth' which they provide for the 'breadth' of national administrative counts and surveys. They give a better sense not just of the growing extent of poverty but also the complex multi-dimensional structure of the phenomenon.

---

[39] Hewlett, 1993

rich and poor

The problem is one of social polarisation, or, as some described it, 'The Growing Divide' [40] and not just growing poverty. The two structural trends are not easy to separate. Among households with children the divergence of income has been more pronounced than for other households. As Table 3 shows, there was a loss of purchasing power between 1979 and the 1990s on the part of the poorest 20 (not 10) per cent of such households, accounting for more than 7 millions in the UK population. At the other extreme, the richest 20 per cent experienced an improvement of more than 50 per cent in income purchasing power.

Table 4 picks out some examples of changes for certain types of households. I have also indicated what the gain or loss amounted to in the intervening years. Table 5 shows the average gain but also shows how much worse is

---

[40] Walker and Walker, 1987

Table 3 **Trends in equivalent weekly income of richest and poorest 20 per cent of households with children at 1995 prices (£)**

Total equivalent weekly disposable income (April 1995 prices)	Poorest 20 per cent	
	1979	*1992–93*
Before housing costs	105	104
After housing costs	88	78

Total equivalent weekly disposable income (April 1995 prices)	Richest 20 per cent	
	1979	*1992–93*
Before housing costs	267	414
After housing costs	232	359

Source: Written answer to Jean Corston, MP, *Hansard*, 18 July 1995, cols 1089–1090

Table 4 Low income trends: Equivalent income per week and loss or gain, at April 1995 prices, of rich and poor households 1979–1992/3

Type of household	Income after housing costs					
	Poorest decile			Richest decile		
	1979 (£)	1992–3 (£)	Loss or gain	1979 (£)	1992–3 (£)	Loss or gain
Single adult	41	34	-364	177	286	+5,824
Couple, no children	75	62	-676	321	520	+10,348
Couple + child of 3	89	73	-832	379	614	+12,220
Couple + child of 16	104	86	-936	443	718	+14,300
Couple + children of 3 & 8	106	88	-936	453	734	+14,612
Couple + children of 3, 8 & 11	126	104	-1,144	536	869	+17,316
Couple + children of 11, 16 & 17	152	126	-1,352	649	1,051	+20,904

Note: The data apply to the median of the decile, not the mean. They apply to weekly income, and are subject to sampling error. The fall in income in each type of household in the poorest tenth of the population also applies when the self-employed are excluded from the analysis. When income is assessed before housing costs there is a similar marked divergence during the 14 years in the incomes of poorest and richest deciles, but the incomes of the poorest households are the same or marginally higher in 1992–3 than 1979 (varying from £0 per week to £2 per week).
Source: Written answer to Jean Corston, MP, *Hansard*, 18 July 1995, cols 1089–1090

Table 5 **Percentage change in real incomes 1979–1992/3 (household income after housing costs, at April 1995 prices)**

Population group	Including self-employed	Excluding self-employed
Total population	+38	+36
Second poorest tenth	+1	+2
Poorest tenth	-17	-10

Source: Hansard, 26 October 1994, cols 691–692

the change in the income of each succeeding tenth of the population below the average.

In picking out the extremes, and comparing the average with the lowest ranks the graduation from one to the other has to be remembered. The structure draws upon the hierarchical wage, occupational and social networks of a thousand institutions. What explains, and what justifies, a nation converting an unequal structure represented by a 4:1 ratio of rich to poor (comparing the disposable incomes of the richest 20 per cent to those of the poorest 20 per cent), to a much more unequal structure represented by a ratio of 7:1 in less than a generation?

This conveys nothing of the mounting wealth of the richest 500. In a regular review the *Sunday Times* explains who they are and how their wealth has grown. It reported on 14 April 1996 that on 1 January they were worth nearly £71 billions, or 28 per cent more than 12 months earlier, with £140 millions each. Privately invested, that wealth would provide interest to cover almost the entire cost of educating the 5 million five to nine year-olds in British primary schools.

The structure of acquisition has become so much more unequal so fast that we are bound to ask more questions. Is the trend acceptable? Where will it end? What are the implications for taxation and the wage system? There seems little rhyme or reason in the observed variation country by country in the distribution. The US and the UK are very similar in degree of inequality. Japan and Sweden are different examples of countries with a much smaller ratio – generally agreed to be nearer 4:1. When I visited Japan in October 1995 I was of course struck by lower rates of unemployment and better wages for most working people. But I was also struck by evidence that the salary or wage rates for the senior administrative and professional classes were relatively lower than in the UK. One culture was manifestly more integrated, more restrained, less divided, and more equitable, than the other. And we must not suppose it is somehow natural or unprovoked. It is related to the binding power of beliefs and values. It is also related to the choice of policies.

In the words of an authoritative inquiry group set up by the Joseph Rowntree Foundation, which included the deputy chairman of the Confederation of British Industry, and which was chaired by Sir Peter Barclay, income inequality has in fact reached 'a higher level than recorded since the war'.[41] This matches a 'universal' international trend, but the change has been faster in the UK than in any other country except New Zealand. As many as 20–30 per cent of the population, or between 12 and 17 millions, 'failed to benefit from economic growth'.[42] Social security slowed the growth of inequality in the early 1980s, but not subsequently. Inequality of post-tax incomes grew as rapidly as that of pre-tax incomes. There have been other 'knock-on' effects. In the 1990s house prices at the lower end of the market have been falling, while those at the

---

[41] Barclay, 1995, p. 6

[42] Barclay, 1995, p. 6

higher end have recovered and are now rising
again. The differences between deprived and
affluent neighbourhoods have widened even
more. And since council housing is grouped in
particular estates, the divergence of income
groups according to tenure has resulted in a
greater concentration of people with low
incomes in particular neighbourhoods.

This evidence supports the introduction at the
earliest possible date of a social development
policy. The object would be to obtain much less
severe structural inequality as well as less
poverty. The two are of course related but there
is mounting scientific and statistical evidence
of the harm both cause.[43] The emerging
pattern of poverty is producing concentrations
of misery and a substantial incidence of
poverty in prosperous and poor areas alike. But
it has ramifications throughout society which
threaten established institutions and cherished
values alike.

---

[43] For example, Wilkinson, 1994

social stability and one nation

The costs of absolute and overall poverty are costs of course to people who find themselves in that situation – including the greater risks of premature mortality, ill-health and disability, the reduction of opportunities to get and keep adequately paid jobs, and also to meet others, travel and fulfil individual hopes and those of their children.

The costs apply to taxpayers who provide benefits for unemployment and Income Support for families, and health services, schools and housing.

But to try to meet these costs is in our own interests too. Few of us have a life-long guarantee of economic security. Indeed, labour market insecurities are affecting more people from bottom to top of the occupational hierarchy. The standards we apply to others may also be those we are obliged to rely on when we encounter unexpected setbacks.

They are also standards we see being applied to members, whether young or old, of our own families. By extension, when they receive their acknowledged benefits we share their satisfaction. These are standards which apply to the groups to which we belong. They will apply to us in turn – and it matters to us whether we see them as acceptable.

This cuts across stereotyped divisions between rich and poor. Wealth is no refuge. It can buy privilege, but the best of those privileges are not easy to protect in an increasingly unstable environment. It is true that rich people incur the extra costs of making their homes and behaviour safe from thieves, but they are also aware that the reduction of poverty weakens the necessity for such action. The removal of poverty is therefore in large measure about the kind of society in which we prefer to live, and therefore the kind of relationships we prefer to encourage and the unnecessary costs we prefer to avoid or prevent. Increasing poverty is not a necessary price of increased prosperity for some, but a damaging cost to all.

causes

The national problem is one also of identifying causes and their proportionate effect. The second volume of the report from the Joseph Rowntree Inquiry Group, by John Hills, provides the best available introduction.[44] There has been a growing income gap between those in and outside employment; a growing proportion of the population without income from employment, and a growth of inequality among those with employment income. Between 1886 and 1973 earnings differentials stayed suprisingly static. That has now changed.

By 1992 wages for the lowest paid were lower in real terms than in 1975; middle-range earnings had grown by 35 per cent, but high wages by more than 50 per cent. The trend has been similar for women and men. There are a variety of institutional factors at work –

---

[44] Hills, 1995 and 1996, and forthcoming; and see Jenkins, 1994, and 1995

including the weakening of trades union bargaining power, the decline of minimum wage regulation, more difficulty than previously for those with few educational qualifications – despite a growth in the proportion in each new generation with such qualifications – and a sharp fall in the earnings and career expectations of young people.

The loss of jobs also provoked growth in self-employment. The fact that such growth resulted in more unequal incomes among the self-employed than among the employed population led in turn to greater overall inequality. The growth of dividend and property income has also contributed substantially to increased inequality of the dispersion. The dispersion of income among pensioners has also widened – partly because of the selective effect of occupational pensions, especially for high-earners, coming to maturity, but also because basic state pensions have been tied to price increases and Income Support has been an ineffective top-up.

One underlying reason for the lag of incomes among poor people generally has been the uprating of benefits year by year according to prices rather than by earnings. The Fowler reforms in social security in the late 1980s have been analysed. The poorest families were supposed to be targeted but in the poorest fifth of the population almost as many families lost as gained by the reforms. [45]

Taxation strategy has not lessened the growth of inequality and has had a virtually neutral effect. The possible growth of revenue from personal income taxation from those becoming prosperous was reduced through cuts in tax rates, but new discretionary indirect taxes drew increased revenue from middle and low income groups. There has not been the merest hint of a rational approach to a fair tax system.

The causes of a deteriorating situation are therefore multiple – to do with the constraints imposed on trades unions, changes in direct

---

[45] Hills, 1995, p. 58

and indirect taxation, changes in the wages system, successive changes in social security, the changing scope and application of investment income, and above all major changes in labour market structure.

I would want to highlight two overriding causes. One is what might be called the 'runaway' destabilising influence of the international market. The other is the ideological drive behind the Government's construction of a range of different economic and social policies. We have to come to terms with both.

ideas towards a strategy

How, therefore, should we try to deal with these multiple but also overriding causes of a deepening national malaise? Britain's economy is hard to disentangle from the global web of trading relations. Like the economies of other countries it can only be assessed in this wider context. That does not mean to say it conforms closely to a fixed pattern. Each country carries a different historical legacy and its mix of institutions is differently placed in relation to the advantages and disadvantages of the international market. But that still means it follows – early or late – broad international trends.

Unemployment is a good example. Since the 1960s and 1970s the rate of unemployment in Europe has more than doubled, as standardised measures from the OECD and others have shown. It would be absurd to suppose that any European country is immune from this trend. Management of companies is no longer what it was. 'Down-sizing' of workforces was established as a long-term phenomenon within national economies. Plants and jobs moved overseas; and jobs at home had to adjust to order-books shrinking because of overseas competition. And public expenditure and the public sector both came under attack.

The international economic culture became one increasingly disdainful of public services and of taxation to support those services, and correspondingly favourable to the privatisation of utilities and services alike.

Britain has not been good at identifying international causes of national and local problems and running them to ground. Much more searching scrutiny of the role of international financial agencies and transnational corporations, collaborative action with different governments to monitor and democratise them, and putting in place appropriate international company laws and institutions to control extortion and excess is required. That is an awesome prospect. But the Copenhagen Summit makes it inescapable, as bodies like

Oxfam[46], Christian Aid, One World Action and Save the Children have tried so valiantly to reveal.

The other overriding cause, I have said, is the ideological drive behind different national economic and social policies. Social scientists are liable to select special areas or subjects for close attention and perhaps overlook their connections and motivating forces. We need to remedy that. If we restrict our vision to recent national history we are conscious of the interplay of the elements of structural change – cuts in the costs of public services, cuts in progressive tax rates, deregulation, legal limitations on the powers of trades unions, privatisation and liberalisation of the wages systems. A more enlightened approach would be to deal systematically with these inter-locking elements.

Of course, the fashioning of a hundred policies and pieces of legislation and the restructuring

---

[46] For example, Oxfam, 1995

of workforces in the public and private sectors lies behind each of those key elements of change. I want to argue that this knowledge can liberate our ideas to contribute to change and not merely depress us with uncomprehending resignation faced with an insidious web of control.

For change at local level depends not just on dutiful implementation but also on the balancing acts of local initiatives and the growth of opinion to soften the harsh effects of particular situations, set standards, and reintroduce ideologies of justice. This is a call to take up intellectual arms.

international action

There are two revealing developments of the last few years and months. One is the almost uncanny resemblance of the course of poverty and inequality internationally with that in the UK. I have already remarked on the similarity of developments during the 1980s and 1990s in the UK and the US. The dismal evidence from the United States is voluminous. [47] It seems that, grudgingly and years afterwards, Britain's other European partners are following suit.

In much of the Third World and especially Eastern Europe poverty and inequality have grown faster. There is an engrossing literature on the failures of 'structural adjustment' programmes, particularly in Africa, and common agreement by the international agencies (for example, UNDP, UNICEF and IFAD) that the share of the poorest countries in

---

[47] For example, Committee on Ways and Means, 1994; Ashworth, Hill and Walker, 1995; Townsend, 1993a

world GDP has fallen. Yet there is little sign of genuine amelioration of civil war, the debt crisis, mass malnutrition and the squeeze on public utilities, and public education and health services. [48]

In areas of the former Soviet Union I have witnessed the descent of swathes of the population into absolute poverty. Part of that process has been due to the deserved collapse of Communist rule. But part is also due to the implacable policies of the IMF and the World Bank [49], and the Group of 7, which have insisted, in their conditions for making loans, on measures which are inappropriate either because they are made too soon, are too extreme, or are too little related to the familiar institutions and current needs of large sections of the population. This is a mark of ideologues who care not for consultation or evidence.

---

[48] Brand, 1994

[49] See, for example, Townsend with Donkor, 1996

It is women and children, the elderly and the sick and disabled who have been submitted to what some in UNICEF have described as 'ultra-poverty'.[50] In important respects we have withdrawn from unwavering allegiance to universal welfare, citizenship and human rights. Britain has cut its overseas aid budget far below the level promised 50 years ago and barely acknowledges any reasoned preparation of priorities in how it is allocated. Our international obligations have to be seen as protective of the standards we expect for ourselves. And people who recognise there is a growing problem in their own backyards are more likely to be sensitive to, and learn from, others who have been in a worse plight for longer.

---

[50] See, in particular, Cornia, 1993, 1994a and 1994b

conclusion

I have tried to explain how serious is the
problem of growing poverty and widening
social inequality in Britain, and that we have
to take more concerted national and international action to halt that process. This amounts
to a call for a national plan to
fulfil the agreement reached in 1995 at the
World Summit on Social Development in
Copenhagen.

National planning is unfashionable. Its absence
implies drift and inconsequential measures
devised by government more to divert national
attention from our real problems than deal
with them successfully. There are problems in
establishing and even recognising priorities.

Perhaps the urgency of our problem can be
illustrated by the collapse and even social
dissolution of some countries into violence and
penury. We can point to those which only a few
short years ago displayed little of the extent or
severity of the conditions to which they have to

submit today. The structural trends have to be understood and predicted.

Nor can we be too confident in the capacity of alternative elected governments to remedy matters. In considering prospects following the next General Election in Britain we are bound to ask whether the problem is not only measured and explained, but related to the policies under active discussion by the politicians. Social reconstruction will not be easy, but it is possible. Britain has substantial resources to call on.

Certainly there are public services and forms of redistribution which can be 'ring-fenced' nationally in the international market by means of government legislation and administration. France and Sweden are examples of countries defending vulnerable sections of their populations more effectively than the UK – with no evident damage to their capacity to achieve a comparable level of economic growth.

There are also possibilities of shrewd and ingenious local measures to assist impoverished groups, extend fellowship and re-ignite hope.

But there is national political responsibility too. An illustration is the stream of surprisingly cautious statements about future policy from the Labour Party. I say cautious because after 17 years the present Government has ensured that Britain's social security system, and particularly its prospective pension costs, are smaller than most of its European counterparts, and there is scope for some measured improvements, especially if initiatives can be taken to reduce unemployment and increase the ✗ number of jobs.

The possible withdrawal of child benefit from 16 to 19-year-olds is a current example. This ✗ was a proposal made in his John Smith Memorial lecture by Gordon Brown, the Shadow Chancellor of the Exchequer. Rather like other proposals to do with a tax on the former public utilities and a possible means-tested complement to a declining basic retirement pension, one is bound to ask sharp questions. As in other instances, no carefully-laid 'plan' seems to have been prepared and circulated.

How would such a development affect the deepening trend of poverty and the widening trend in the dispersion of income? How does it rate in the ranking of structural priorities for the next Government? Might it represent the thin end of a nasty wedge for the rest of child benefit, and universal benefits generally? Might it be the wrong kind of signal to send out to women and families with children – many of them shown here and elsewhere to have experienced a sharp fall in real income? And does it not overlook the history of its adoption nationally – with general agreement – as an allowance of which part represented a payment in lieu of child tax relief? Would not prosperous families have a strong case for the reintroduction of child tax allowances so that they were not taxed as heavily as couples without dependent children?

I ask such questions because an incoming government has the choice of either conforming to the worst international practice – and continuing the winding down of public expenditure, encouraging inequality, paving the way for lower-paid jobs, gradually abandoning universal benefits and privatising public services and pensions, or insisting on better minimum national standards for wages, benefits and public sector services.

The former is fatalistic, and merely accepts the fact that millions in the population, and many more millions overseas, are on a slippery slope from which there is no realistic escape. So, it is argued, we cannot influence what is inevitable. We can only make the best of a bad job.

The latter is a kind of insurance policy for our own future, for stability, and a more secure world for our children. It will involve uncomfortable national arguments between the haves and the have-nots, and even more difficult international arguments with the IMF, the World Bank and the increasingly powerful representatives of transnational corporations intent on freeing their mode of operations at others' expense. But maybe in the process of argument, and determined international action to introduce what might be called the beginnings of an 'international welfare state' they too can be encouraged to accept terms of responsibility.

So what specific policies have to be put in place? The priority has to be an international plan of campaign. Before his death in 1994 John Smith, the former leader of the Labour Party, argued for the reconstruction of international agencies like the World Bank and the International Monetary Fund. Others have called for similar action. No doubt reorganisation of the UN itself is also implied, with devolution of power from the G7 countries and particularly from the United States. Democratisation and accountability of the international agencies might begin the slow process of bringing social development to the heart of the policy goals of the international agencies.

These objectives could not be achieved, however, without determined collaborative international action to regulate multi-national companies, and especially to reconstruct international company law. That would mean laying a common basis for taxation and control of market monopolies across the world. Governments will have to embrace a new internationalism rather than the desperate, resigned or murderous forms of nationalism which are driving current polarisation and social self-destruction. And non-government organisations will have to give most of their time to the achievement of a common international framework of trade, much higher environmental and social standards, and a more extensive pattern of public services which satisfy basic human needs.

Nationally both employment and income distribution have to be transformed. Limits will need to be set on high earnings and levels of personal wealth, just as a statutory minimum level of earnings will have to be introduced. A minimally adequate level of benefit for the non-employed will also have to be promoted strenuously, and financed.

In the UK contributory national insurance already exists and can be modernised to cover new insecurities in the labour market and the heavy costs of child care and care of disabled and infirm elderly people. Perhaps the most important step (because it affects the livelihood of the whole population in their retirement years) will be to restore the link between earnings and the annual uprating of the basic retirement pension, but also strengthen the State Earnings Related Pension scheme, which has been unnecessarily dismembered in the last ten years.

People under the age of 40 sometimes forget that long-established public institutions – like social insurance – were introduced originally not only to create opportunities which otherwise would not exist for people on low incomes to climb out of poverty, but also to provide long-term personal security for people at every level of income as well. Financial adversity can strike unexpectedly and comprehensive state systems designed to provide a minimum fall-back income have always been popular. Universal contributions – and benefits – also establish a strong foundation for economic growth and social stability, and are easier to adapt to modern needs than half-baked, poorly explained and inequitable private sector substitutes.

Better basic and additional state pensions are in fact the key elements of a general strategy to slow down and then reverse worsening poverty and inequality. They comprise the central element of the infrastructure of social security. If they can be strengthened then other policies to strengthen the incomes of those who are disabled, sick, unemployed, maintaining and caring for children, and caring for dependent disabled and elderly people also become feasible.

Personal security is inseperable from collective security, and collective insurance is the most acceptable method yet devised of pursuing both objectives in the national interest – being administratively the cheapest and simplest and economically the most efficient of the institutions on offer.

Such a package of policies depends first on a range of taxes, contributions and income-generating rules which are essentially *redistributive*. The redistribution is from independent to dependent parts of the lifetime of the individual and not just from rich to poor. That is a principle backed by a majority of the population and which deserves to be upheld and spelt out clearly by any incoming government. In any practical sense, 'redistribution' in the Britain of the mid-1990s is something of a joke.

An effective policy package also depends on consistent advocacy of better and more extensive public services. Public health, education, housing, community care and transport services have to be greatly improved. Again, all available evidence shows that this commands the support of the great majority of the public. It also makes sense because we live in families and communities of people belonging to three and four generations and have a high appreciation of what common national standards and rights can do for the untried as well as the handicapped.

No one can be under any illusion that these structural changes can be brought about quickly. Two five-year programmes at least will be required. What counts is a change of direction that can be measured and becomes indisputable. This will inspire trust and confidence.

These developments depend above all on a determined and creative package of policies to increase levels of employment – not only through direct government investment in X selected industries and larger conditional grants for employment creation, but also a plan for larger numbers to be employed in the public services. That is an inescapable lesson of the continuing high levels of long-term unemployment – predicted by the OECD to rise to even higher levels in Europe. As numerous studies show, much of the cost of such an expansion would be defrayed by the consequential reduction of the costs of paying benefits to millions of the unemployed and prematurely retired, and the large sums generated in additional tax revenues.

I conclude that whatever our hopes of an incoming government there is no escape from the collaborative mobilisation of representative opinion to press for more concerted, and coherent, national and local action to attack poverty. Planning can help to provide packages of policies to construct change rather than leave the field to competitive destruction.

afterword

The UK is skidding even faster than other countries down the slippery slope of increasing poverty and inequality. At the end of summer 1996 there are a mounting number of reports confirming the trend which has been the theme of this book. The Government of John Major is making even greater efforts to deny this structural change in society and disclaim all responsibility. Thus, the United Nations Development Programme (UNDP) finds that the gap between the richest and poorest 20 per cent of population has continued to widen and that the trend in the UK has been faster than in any other industrial country, with the exception of New Zealand. Inequality here is now as extreme as it is in Nigeria.[51]

Three acts by the Secretary of State for Social Services, Peter Lilley, betray the Government's intention to conceal the deteriorating situation.

---

[51] UNDP, 1996

First, a July 1996 statistical report prepared at the DSS and designed to improve information about people with low income dodges all the key questions. In 207 pages the report of the 1994–95 *Family Resources Survey* gives nothing away. Perhaps because it was found to contain little of interest it was ignored by the press.

The report contains nothing about the distribution of income after tax among the poorest and richest 10 or 20 per cent of the population. Nor about changes in the real living standards of unemployed and low paid people and one parent families. Nothing of consequence is revealed about the 33 per cent of the sample who did not answer the survey questions. Worst of all, children, who have been most at risk of serious deprivation in the last 17 years, attract no special report. Nowhere do we learn what are their real living standards in different structural situations.[52] The survey costs the taxpayer a small fortune to conduct. It is

---

[52] Semmence et al, 1996

difficult to open the report and believe that DSS statisticians are allowed any professional independence to prepare meaningful evidence.

Second, the annual *Households Below Average Income* report, usually published each July, has been delayed, probably until at least November 1996. Despite its omissions and questionable style of analysis, perhaps ministers feel it still reveals more than they want to admit about low incomes.

Third, the conclusions of a research report from the DSS have been misrepresented. Peter Lilley claimed that the research had 'blown apart' the idea that the poor had got poorer under the Tories. The trouble is that it does no such thing. The research turns out to be a working paper and a very incomplete and flimsy piece of work at that.[53] It does not cover a cross-section of the entire population, but only males between 25 and 44 in the poorest

---

[53] Ball and Marland, 1996; and see also Timmins N., 'Fewer Poor – A Tall Tory Tale?', *The Independent*, 30 June 1996

tenth of earners traced by means of national insurance records from 1978 to 1992. More than a third of this group stopped paying contributions, presumably because they dropped out of work and lost income, and are not included in the results. If they had been included the small average gain in real income claimed for the group as a whole during a period of 14 years by Mr Lilley might have been a loss. Certainly the research poses questions rather than providing answers.

Since 1979 the composition of the poorest 10 per cent of the population has changed. More are lone parent families and are unemployed, and fewer are pensioners. Some have moved into higher income groups, just as others in higher groups have fallen into the poorest group. And by limited indicators – like ownership of telephones and video recorders – it seems that even the poorest groups in the population are better off. But such indicators are misleading if they are not balanced by information about the loss by households of free and subsidised public services, including opthalmology, dental treatment, libraries, playing fields and leisure centres, school meals and a worsening of home and environmental conditions in some places. More of a balance sheet of losses and gains on the part of the poorest tenth or fifth of the population has to be devised, as well as an account offered of the changing pattern of basic material and social needs in relation to income.

What happens to people in particular situations over a number of years is of enormous interest. It can of course affect our interpretation of information we have been given about rich and poor at the beginning and end of that period of years. But we also have to remember that prosperous people can slide into poverty, that free and subsidised goods and services may have to be paid for, or cost more, or even fade out of existence. Some problems diminish, others, like homelessness, multiply or newly appear. Mr Lilley's selective, and frankly superficial, social research programme is no substitute for a comprehensive scientific research programme.

During 1996 there have, however, also been two other significant developments. A coalition has been formed of non-government organisations to demand some response from the Government to the plan agreed at the Copenhagen Summit in 1995. Ninety-three organisations – including Christian Aid, Oxfam, Save the Children, Barnados, the Low Pay Unit, the Child Poverty Action Group, Church Action Against Poverty and many more – had joined the coalition by July 1996, and were intensifying the pressure on Peter Lilley and John Major. There comes a point, of course, when the sheer volume of public, and scientific, pressure becomes too great for Government ministers to ignore.

The second development is equally significant. The tide of monetarism seems to be on the turn. During the 1970s the arguments for liberalisation, privatisation, cuts in public services, cuts in personal income taxes, restraints on collective bargaining and reductions in wages and conditions of employment, and deregulation, gathered momentum. Margaret

Thatcher was a leading exponent of this and in the 1980s Britain became a crucible for the monetarist experiment.

The international agencies supported that argument during the 1980s on the grounds that this was the only way that economic growth could be sustained, and the social costs of that growth defrayed by 'trickle-down'. They persisted with 'structural adjustment' programmes in Third World countries, brutal liberalisation programmes in Eastern Europe and the republics of the former Soviet Union, and rather less savage programmes of cuts in public expenditure, deregulation and privatisation in the most prosperous industrial countries, including the United Kingdom. The third package of policies is still being urged on richer countries in Europe, like the UK, and elsewhere. In April 1996, for example, the IMF continued to call for reduced spending on welfare. [54] The British Treasury seems to be eager to comply – judging by the leaked

---

[54] *The Guardian*, 18 April 1996

Treasury paper *Strategic Considerations for the Treasury 2000–2006.* [55]

The IMF has, however, become isolated in recent months. Other bodies have begun to raise different arguments. The World Bank was clearly on the defensive at the 1995 Copenhagen Summit about its Structural Adjustment Programmes and has begun to soften recommended strategies for 'targeting'. Governments of some European countries, like those of the Netherlands and Sweden, have begun to fight back and develop sophisticated defences of their welfare state policies. They have issued briefs and research papers which are in a different class to many of those produced by the staff of the World Bank and the IMF. Some of this work has exposed the crude monetarist ideology of the international finance agencies, and their failure to examine the key structural role in different countries of the public sector of the economy and of the public services in general.

---

[55] *The Guardian*, 17 July 1996

International agencies like the OECD and UNDP have begun to emphasise the fact that minimum wages, strong trade unions and generous welfare benefits help to defend the social fabric of industrialised nations against the corrosive impact of growing wage inequality [56] and actually strengthen, rather than weaken, economic prospects.

One example of the remarkable change of professional and political mood is a report on privatisation from the UN Conference on Trade and Development. [57] This is favourably disposed towards privatisation but in fact is full of doubts and lessons about failures. Evidence of the successes of privatisation is often non-existent or, at best, very shaky. When tracking examples the role historically and contemporaneously of the public sector proves not to have been examined and has clearly been underestimated. Grudgingly, the new report concedes that a much larger role for it in future

---

[56] See, for example, the OECD's annual *World Employment Outlook*, 1996; and UNDP, 1996

[57] UNCTAD, 1995

has to be acknowledged.

Thus, the privatisation of pensions in Chile resulted in 4.1 million workers (86 per cent of the total labour force) being 'affiliated' to the new system by 1991 but only 2.5 million of these (or 52 per cent) were contributors, because of 'loss of jobs, lack of incentives, late payment by employers of the employee contributions collected by them and a high proportion of independent, informal workers, together with a high incidence of poverty'.[58] Accumulating information now showed that 'an important proportion [of contributors] will end up with acquired benefits less than the guaranteed minimum'. High marketing costs were 'making the commissions more expensive than they need to be'. Transitional costs of changing the structure had been heavy and the effects on the total volume of savings was unclear. Exclusion from membership was becoming a burning issue. These criticisms are familiar to historians of the debates that have

---

[58] UNCTAD, 1995, p. 204

taken place about private social services.

The general conclusion reached in the report is that both pay-as-you-go schemes and individual capitalisation schemes have their place in future planning. 'A hybrid pension system could attempt to combine their respective strengths, while avoiding some of their weaknesses.' [59] One alternative, they say, would be a pension system closely supervised by the state which would include three tiers. The first tier would be a universal defined-benefits pay-as-you-go system, with flat-rate and earnings-related components, jointly providing 30–40 per cent of average earnings. A second tier would be represented by a 'compulsorily defined contributions individual capitalisation pension scheme', and a third tier would be made up of voluntary contributions to secure a higher total replacement rate of previous earnings.

These are all hopeful signs of a possible change of direction in the management of the world's

---

[59] UNCTAD, 1995, p. 210

economies. I suspect it will be a few years before the number of dissenting reports gathers such a momentum that real change is conceded. Regrettably, forms of impoverishment, social instability, obscene inequalities and civil war may for a time continue to increase. Many different organisations and professions will have to be mobilised if current trends are to be comprehensively opposed and then changed.

In the United Kingdom an alternative, more desirable and more effective, plan of social campaign must now be worked out urgently.

Despite calls during the mid-1990s such a plan does not yet exist even in rough outline. In some respects this is because of political timidity, in others because of political obduracy. There are affordable, proven policies which can begin gradually to lessen the unequal distribution of income, increase employment, improve the public social services and contribute to a stable international environment. If they are not put together the future will indeed be poorer for Britain.

references

Ashworth K., Hill M. and Walker R. (1995), *The Severity and Duration of Childhood Poverty in the USA*, Loughborough, Centre for Research in Social Policy

Atkinson A.B. and Micklewright J. (1992), *The Distribution of Income in Eastern Europe*, WSP/72, The Welfare State Programme, Suntory-Toyota International Centre for Economics and Related Disciplines, London School of Economics

Baker W. (1989), *Poverty in Birmingham: A Profile*, prepared for the Urban Policy Team, Birmingham Development Department, Birmingham, Birmingham City Council

Ball J. and Marland M. (1996), *Male Earnings Mobility in the Lifetime Labour Market Database*, Working Paper 1, London, Department of Social Security

Barclay Sir P. (1995), *Income and Wealth*, volume 1, York, Joseph Rowntree Memorial Foundation

Benzeval M., Judge K. and Solomon M. (1992), *The Health Status of Londoners: A Comparative Perspective*, London, King's Fund

Benzeval M., Judge K. and Whitehead M. (1995), *Tackling Inequalities in Health: An Agenda for Action*, London, Kings Fund

Berthoud R. and Kempson E. (1992), *Credit and Debt: The PSI Report*, London, Policy Studies Institute

Botting B. ed. (1995), *The Health of Our Children: Decennial Supplement*, The Registrar General's Supplement for England and Wales, OPCS Series DS No. 11, London, HMSO

Bradshaw J. (1990), *Child Poverty and Deprivation in the UK*, special sub-series: *Child Poverty in Industrialised Countries*, UNICEF International Child Development Centre, Innocenti Occasional Papers No. 8, Florence, Italy, UNICEF

Bradshaw J. (1996), *Budget Standards for the United Kingdom*, Aldershot, Avebury

Bradshaw J. and Holmes H. (1989), *Living on the Edge*, London, Tyneside Poverty Action Group

Bradshaw J., Kennedy S., Kilkey M., Hutton S., Corden A., Eardley T., Holmes H. and Neale J. (1996), *The Employment of Lone Parents: A Comparison of Policy in 20 Countries*, London, Family Policy Studies Centre

Brand H. (1994), 'The World Bank, the Monetary Fund, and Poverty', *International Journal of Health Services*, 24, 3, pp. 567–578

Canter D., et al (1995), *The Faces of Homelessness in London*, Aldershot, Dartmouth Publishing

Central Statistical Office (1995), *Social Trends* 1995 edition, London, HMSO

Citro C.F. and Michael R.T. eds. (1995), *Measuring Poverty: A New Approach*, Washington DC, National Academy Press

Cohen R., Coxhall J., Craig G. and Sadiq-Sangster A.S. (1992), *Hardship in Britain: Being Poor in the 1990s*, London, Child Poverty Action Group

Commission of the European Communities (1991), *Final Report on the Second European Poverty Programme 1985–1989*, Luxembourg, Office for the Official Publications of the European Communities

Committee on Ways and Means (1994), *1994 Green Book*, Washington DC, US Government Printing Office

Cornia G. A. (1993), *Public Policy and Social Conditions*; Central and Eastern Europe in transition, Regional Monitoring Report Number 1, Florence, UNICEF

Cornia G.A. (1994a), 'Poverty, Food Consumption, and Nutrition During the Transition to the Market Economy in Eastern Europe', American Economic Association Papers and Proceedings, May, pp.297–303

Cornia G. A. (1994b), *Crisis in Mortality, Health and Nutrition*, Central and Eastern Europe in Transition; public policy and social conditions, Regional Monitoring Report Number 2, Florence, UNICEF

Corston J. (1994), 'Written Answers to Parliamentary Questions about Low Income (collected set)', *Hansard*, 26 October 1994, cols. 689–703

Craig G. and Glendinning C. (1990), *1. The Impact of Social Security Changes: The Views of Families Living in Disadvantaged Areas; 2. The Views of Families Using Barnado*

Pre-School Services; and 3. The Views of Young People, Ilford, Essex, Barnado's Research and Development Section

DHSS (1988a), *Low Income Statistics*, Report of a Technical Review, London, Department of Health and Social Security

DHSS (1988b), *The Measurement of Living Standards for Households Below Average Income, Reply by the Government to the Fourth Report from the Select Committee on Social Services*, Cm 523, London, HMSO

DSS (1990a), *Households Below Average Income: A Statistical Analysis 1981–87*, London, Government Statistical Service, July

DSS (1990b), *The Measurement of Living Standards for Households Below Average Income*, Cm 1162, London, HMSO

DSS (1991), *Households Below Average Income: Stocktaking Report of a Working Group*, London, Department of Social Security

DSS (1994), *Households Below Average Income: A Statistical Analysis 1979–1991/92*, London, HMSO

DSS (1995a), *Households Below Average Income: A Statistical Analysis 1979–1992/93*, London, HMSO

DSS (1995b), *Low Income Statistics: Low Income Families 1989–1992*, Cm 2871, London, HMSO

Eurostat (1990), *Poverty in Figures: Europe in the Early 1980s*, Luxembourg, Office for Official Publications of the European Communities

Eurostat (1994), *Poverty Statistics in the Late 1980s: Research Based on Micro-Data*, Luxembourg, Office for Official Publications of the European Communities

Figueiredo J. B. and Shaheed Z. (1995), *Reducing Poverty through Labour Market Policies*, Geneva, International Institute for Labour Studies

Gaudier M. (1995), *Poverty, Inequality, Exclusion: new approach to theory and practice*, Geneva, International Institute for Labour Studies

Ghai D. and Hewitt de Alcantara C. (1994), *Globalisation and Social Integration; patterns and processes*, Occasional Paper Number 2, World Summit for Social Development, Geneva, UNRISD

References

Gilmour, Sir I. (1992), *Dancing with Dogma*, an autobiography, London, Simon and Schuster

Gordon D. and Pantazis C. (1995), *Breadline Britain in the 1990s: a Report to the Joseph Rowntree Foundation*, York, Joseph Rowntree Foundation

Grayson L., Hobson M. and Smith B., eds. (1992), *INLOGOV Informs on Poverty*, University of Birmingham, Institute of Local Government Studies

Harloe M. (1995), *The People's Home*, Oxford, Blackwell

Hewitt de Alcantara C. (1994), *Structural Adjustment in a Changing World*, Geneva, UNRISD

Hewlett S.A. (1993), *Child Neglect in Rich Nations*, Florence, Italy, and New York, UNICEF

Hills J. (1995), *Income and Wealth*, Vol. 2, York, Joseph Rowntree Foundation

Holtermann S. (1995), *All Our Futures: The Impact of Public Expenditure and Fiscal Policies on Children and Young People*, London, Barnados

Jenkins S.P. (1995), *Assessing Income Distribution Trends: What Lessons from the UK?*, Working Paper No. 95–119 of the ESRC Research Centre on Micro-social Change, Colchester, University of Essex

Johnson P. and Webb S. (1990a), *Low Income Families, 1979–87*, London, Institute of Fiscal Studies

Johnson P. and Webb S. (1990b), *Poverty in Official Statistics: Two Reports*, IFS Commentary No. 24, London, The Institute for Fiscal Studies, October

Kempson E. (1996), *Life on a Low Income*, York, Joseph Rowntree Foundation

Kempson E., Bryson A. and Rowlandson K. (1994), *Hard Times? How Poor Families Make Ends Meet*, London, Policy Studies Institute

Kumar (1993), *Poverty and Inequality in the UK: The Effects on Children*, London, National Children's Bureau

Lee P. and Townsend P. (1994), 'A Study of Inequality, Low Incomes and Unemployment in London, 1985–1992' *International Labour Review*, 133, pp. 579–595

References

Mack J. and Lansley S. (1985), *Poor Britain*, London, Allen and Unwin

Marsh A. and McKay S. (1993), *Families, Work and Benefits*, London, Policy Studies Institute

Meereboer M-T. ed.(1994), *Social (In)Security and Poverty as Global Issues, Poverty and Development*: Analysis and Policy No. 10, the Hague, Ministry of Foreign Affairs, Development Cooperation Information Department

Moore J. (1989), *The End of the Line for Poverty*, London, Conservative Political Centre

Newman B.A. and Thompson R.J. (1989), 'Economic Growth and Social Development: A Longitudinal Analysis of Causal Priority,' *World Development*, pp. 461–471

Nissel M. (1995), 'Social Trends and Social Change', *Journal of the Royal Statistical Society*

Oldfield N. (1992), *Using Budget Standards to Estimate the Cost of Children*, Working Paper No. 15, Family Budget Unit, University of York

Oppenheim C. (1990a), *Holes in the Safety Net*, London, Child Poverty Action Group

Oppenheim C. (1990b), 'Count Me Out: Losing the Poor in the Numbers Game', *Poverty*, Journal of the Child Poverty Action Group, No. 76, Summer, pp. 11–14

Oppenheim C. and Harker L. (1996), *Poverty: The Facts*, revised and updated 3rd edition, London, Child Poverty Action Group

Osberg L. (ed.) (1991), *Economic Inequality and Poverty: International Perspectives*, New York and London, Sharpe

Oxfam (1995), *Poverty Report*, Oxford, Oxfam

Robbins D. (1994), *Observatory on National Policies to Combat Social Exclusion*, Third Annual Report, Commission of the European Communities, Directorate V for Employment, Social Affairs and Industrial Relations, Lille, EEIG

Rodgers G. (1995), *New Approaches to Poverty Analysis and Policy – II: The Poverty Agenda and the ILO: issues for research and action*, Geneva, International Institute for Labour Studies

Rodgers G. and van der Hoeven R. (1995), *New Approaches to Poverty Analysis and Policy – III: The Poverty Agenda: trends and policy options*, Geneva, International Institute for Labour Studies

Rodgers G., Gore, C. and Figueiredo J. B. (1994), *Social Exclusion: rhetoric, reality, responses*, Geneva, International Institute for Labour Studies

Semmence J., Cockerham J., Easto V., Harder H., Fincham P., Hall P., Phillips M., and Bode A. (1996), *Family Resources Survey: Great Britain 1994–95*, London, HMSO

Simpson S. and Dorling D. (1994), 'Those Missing Millions: Implications for Social Statistics of Non-response to the 1991 Census', *Journal of Social Policy* 23, pp. 543–567

Sinfield A., ed. (1993), *Poverty, Inequality and Justice*, New Waverley Papers, Social Policy Series No. 6, University of Edinburgh

Smeeding T. S., O'Higgins M., Rainwater L. and Atkinson A. B. (1989), *Poverty, Inequality and Income Distribution in Comparative Perspective*, London, Simon and Schuster

Social Security Committee (1991), *Low Income Statistics: Households Below Average Income Tables* 1988, First Report, Session 1990–91, House of Commons 401, London, HMSO

Social Services Committee (1988), *Families on Low Income: Low Income Statistics,* Fourth Report, Session 1987–88, House of Commons 565, London HMSO

Social Services Committee (1989), *Minimum Income,* Memoranda laid before the Committee, Session 1988–89, House of Commons 579, London, HMSO

Sparks C. ed. (1995), *Factfile '95,* Rochester, NCH Action for Children

Townsend P. (1991a), *The Poor are Poorer: A Statistical Report on Changes in the Living Standards of Rich and Poor in the United Kingdom, 1979–1989,* No. 1, Bristol Statistical Monitoring Unit, University of Bristol, Department of Social Policy

Townsend P. (1991b), *Meaningful Statistics on Poverty 1991,* No. 2, Bristol Statistical Moniotoring Unit, University of Bristol, Department of Social Policy

References

Townsend P. and Gordon D. (1992), *Unfinished Statistical Business on Low Incomes? A Review of New Proposals by the Department of Social Security for the Production of Public Information on Poverty*, No. 3, Bristol Statistical Monitoring Unit, University of Bristol, Department of Social Policy

Townsend P. (1993a), *The International Analysis of Poverty*, Hemel Hempstead, Harvester Wheatsheaf

Townsend P. (1993b), 'The Repressive Nature and Extent of Poverty in the UK: Predisposing Cause of Crime', Symposium on the Link Between Poverty and Crime, Proceedings of the 11th Annual Conference of the Howard League on 'Poverty and Crime', 8th–10th September, 1993. Summary in *Criminal Justice*, the magazine of the Howard League, 11, 4 (October)

Townsend P. (1994), 'The Need for a New International Poverty Line,' in Gordon D. and Pantazis C. eds., *Breadline Britain*, York, the Joseph Rowntree Foundation

Townsend P., with Donkor K. (1996), *Global Restructuring and Social Policy: The Need to Establish an International Welfare State*, Bristol, Policy Press

UK Research and Development Unit (Local Government Centre, University of Warwick) (1992), *The Poverty Summit: The Edinburgh Declaration*, an agenda for change prepared by participants in the 'Poverty Summit' held in Edinburgh, 6–8 December, 1992

UN (1995), *The Copenhagen Declaration and Programme of Action: World Summit for Social Development 6–12 March 1995*, New York, Unied Nations Department of Publications

UN (1996), 'Special Issue on the Social Summit, Copenhagen, 6–12 March 1995', *Social Policy and Social Progress*, a review published by the United Nations, Vol. 1, No. 1, New York, UN Department of Publications

UNCTAD (1995), *Comparative Experiences with Privatisation: Policy Insights and Lessons Learned*, New York and Geneva

UNDP (1995), *Human Development Report 1994*, New York and Oxford, Oxford University Press

UNDP (1996), *Human Development Report 1995*, New York and Oxford, Oxford University Press

UNRISD (1995a), *States of Disarray: the social effects of globalisation*, an UNRISD Report for the World Summit for Social Development, Geneva, UNRISD

UNRISD (1995b), *Adjustment, Globalisation and Social Development*, Report of the UNRISD/UNDP International Seminar on Economic Restructuring and Social Policy, New York, January 1995, Geneva, UNRISD

Van Bueren G. (1994), *The International Law on the Rights of the Child*, Cambridge, Mass., Kluwer Law International

Walker C. and Walker A. (1987), *The Growing Divide*, London, Child Poverty Action Group

Whiteford P. (1985), *A Family's Needs: Equivalence Scales, Poverty and Social Security*, Research Paper No. 27, Development Division, Department of Social Security, Canberra

Wilkinson R.G. (1994), *Unfair Shares: The Effects of Widening Income Differences on the Welfare of the Young*, Ilford, Essex, Barnado's

World Bank (1990), *World Development Report 1990: Poverty*, Washington DC, World Bank

World Bank (1993), *Implementing the World Bank's Strategy to Reduce Poverty: Progress and Challenges*, Washington DC, World Bank

World Bank (1995a), *Advancing Social Development: a World Bank contribution to the Social Summit*, Washington DC, World Bank

World Bank (1995b), *Investing in People: the World Bank in Action*, Washington DC, World Bank

index

A Poor Future